First published in 2020 by
Clarity Media Ltd
www.clarity-media.co.uk

Puzzles created by Dan Moore
Design and layout by Andy Harwood

About Clarity Media

Clarity Media are a leading provider of a huge range of puzzles for adults and children. For more information on our services, please visit us at www.pzle.co.uk. For information on purchasing puzzles for publication, visit us at www.clarity-media.co.uk

Puzzle Magazines

If you enjoy the puzzles in this book, then you may be interested in our puzzle magazines. We have a very large range of magazines that you can download and print yourself in PDF format at our Puzzle Magazine site. For more information, take a look at www.puzzle-magazine.com

Online Puzzles

If you prefer to play puzzles online, please take a look at the Puzzle Club website, at www.thepuzzleclub.com

**We also have more puzzle books available at
www.puzzle-book.co.uk**

Puzzle 1

Across

1 - England's flowers (5)

4 - Purple red drooping flowers (7)

7 - Eg apples and pears (5)

8 - Placing shrubs in the ground (8)

9 - Science of numbers (5)

11 - Chicken will crack this (8)

15 - Eg frogs and newts (8)

17 - Not old (5)

19 - Warmth needed for growth (8)

20 - Give out (5)

21 - Serves no purpose (7)

22 - Makes comfortable (5)

Down

1 - Red summer fruit (9)

2 - Unusual (7)

3 - Minimal outline of the facts (7)

4 - These seeds served with fish (6)

5 - Like eg sage thyme (6)

6 - From Eire (5)

10 - Tool for cutting back (9)

12 - Symbol of Scotland (7)

13 - Very clear (7)

14 - Comes each year (6)

16 - Dull purples (6)

18 - Sponge used by flower arrangers (5)

Puzzle 2

Across

1 - Poisonous yellow flowered tree (8)

5 - Not wanted in the garden (4)

8 - Gorse (5)

9 - South African area (5)

10 - ___ artichoke; vegetable (5)

11 - Suitable name for a flower grower? (5)

12 - Digging implement (5)

17 - Beneath (5)

18 - Man-made fibre (5)

19 - Solve (anag) (5)

20 - Flat green part of a plant (4)

21 - Forget-me-not (8)

Down

1 - Celery flavoured herb (6)

2 - Pandas like this (6)

3 - Summer climbing legumes (6,5)

4 - Province in Northern Ireland (6)

6 - Covers up potatoes (6)

7 - Clear out the pond (6)

8 - Types of roses (11)

12 - Hovels (anag) (6)

13 - Rhododendron like plant (6)

14 - Leaf stalk eaten raw or cooked (6)

15 - Season before Christmas (6)

16 - Spring flowering bulb (6)

Puzzle 3

Across

1 - ___ on the cob (4)

3 - Creating a lawn (8)

9 - Underground root stem (7)

10 - Heather (5)

11 - The space above (3)

12 - Needed to tie up plants (5)

15 - An area covered by 10A (5)

16 - British Broadcasting Corporation (abbrev) (3)

17 - Measuring device (5)

18 - Stinking iris; dig lawn (anag) (7)

19 - N Madeira (anag) (8)

20 - Curved structure (4)

Down

1 - National flower of Japan (13)

2 - Rather wet (5)

4 - Sad or regretful (6)

5 - Biennial flower chosen by Billy? (5,7)

6 - A beginning (7)

7 - Plant of the genus Muscari (5,8)

8 - Deciduous flowering shrub (4,2,6)

13 - Farm vehicle (7)

14 - Measured the capacity (6)

16 - Garden summer-house (5)

Puzzle 4

Across

1 - Purple flowering autumn corm (8)

5 - Crocus and daffodil come from this (4)

8 - Queen's Race course (5)

9 - A gift (7)

10 - Alpine plants look good here (7)

12 - The prop (anag) (7)

14 - Beautiful evenings (7)

16 - Very overgrown garden might need this (7)

18 - Form of marjoram (7)

19 - Inside (5)

20 - Where the sun rises (4)

21 - ___ goose: form of limpet (8)

Down

1 - Heavy soil (4)

2 - ___ spit: evidence of the froghopper (6)

3 - Jerusalem or globe (9)

4 - Alan Titchmarsh is this (6)

6 - Not level (6)

7 - Disease of grapes (8)

11 - Flower for your buttonhole (9)

12 - Yellow spring flower (8)

13 - Disabled ___: needed by public gardens (6)

14 - Spanish lady (6)

15 - Tin che (anag) (6)

17 - Eg elm or oak (4)

Puzzle 5

Across

1 - Red flowered plant popular at Christmas (10)

6 - Elegant and refined (4)

7 - The flower of the lotus plant (5)

8 - On time (6)

11 - Soil (5)

12 - Stare (anag) (5)

14 - Mayonnaise seasoned with garlic (5)

15 - Grown for bread flour (5)

17 - Variety of African violet and star sign (5)

19 - Act as one (6)

21 - Needed for cutting in the garden (5)

22 - Oval shaped fruit (4)

23 - Removed old flowers (10)

Down

1 - Tropical melon shaped fruit (6)

2 - Antirrhinum (10)

3 - What you can do with 13D (4)

4 - ___ Roddick; Bodyshop founder (5)

5 - Shrub of the mallow family (8)

9 - How plant roots absorb water (7)

10 - Evergreen plant of the vinca family (10)

13 - Tool used to tidy edges (8)

16 - Piece of cotton (6)

18 - Protect (5)

20 - The corn lily (4)

Puzzle 6

Across

1 - Fluid for growth in plants (3)

3 - Green vegetable from a pod (3)

5 - Area adjoining a house (5)

8 - Pick what you've sown (4)

9 - Brandy (8)

11 - Edible plant grown in water (10)

13 - Bulbous blue-flowered plant (6)

14 - Nut of the tree prunus dulcis (6)

17 - Type of perennial flowering plant (10)

21 - Welcome insect (8)

22 - ___weed;climbing plant often a weed (4)

23 - Step (5)

24 - Tool with toothed blade (3)

25 - Deciduous tree with serrate leaves (3)

Down

1 - Cereal stems (5)

2 - No gardener wants this weed (8)

4 - The light seen at dawn (6)

5 - Large yellowish fruit (5)

6 - A fork has 3 of these (4)

7 - Where apple trees grow (7)

10 - Verbal (4)

12 - Establish plants in an area (8)

13 - Small onion (7)

15 - Good fortune (4)

16 - Candytuft is a plant of this genus (6)

18 - Fix firmly in the ground (5)

19 - Popular succulent plant (5)

20 - Axe-like tool (4)

Puzzle 7

Across

1 - Plant that lives for 1 year (6)

4 - Eg bee; butterfly or frog (6)

9 - Type of cherry (7)

10 - Time for resolutions! (3,4)

11 - Metal fastenings (5)

12 - Type of daisy (5)

14 - Founded on (5)

15 - Garden string (5)

17 - Small group of trees (5)

18 - Deadly plant (7)

20 - Subtropical shrub of the verbena family (7)

21 - Inhabitant of Central Italian region (6)

22 - Thin bladed mowing tool (6)

Down

1 - Nut of the tree prunus dulcis (6)

2 - Daffodils (8)

3 - Collection of maps (5)

5 - Very tall tree (7)

6 - Where bees live (4)

7 - Educational qualification (6)

8 - Fragrant climbing plant (11)

13 - The aubergine (8)

14 - Popular annual in the garden (7)

15 - Casual wear (1-5)

16 - Open ___: seed used as food (6)

17 - Shaped like an ice cream holder (5)

19 - Green boggy plant not wanted in the lawn (4)

Puzzle 8

Across

1 - Ideal bud (anag) (8)

5 - Lemon___; fragrant herb (4)

7 - Herb used in Italian cooking (5)

8 - Root vegetable (5)

10 - Masticating food (7)

12 - An advantage (7)

14 - Secured a plant (6)

16 - Used as a nutrient provider (7)

19 - Type of hazelnut (7)

20 - Musical drama (5)

21 - Makes prostrate (4)

22 - Pungently aromatic low growing herbs (6)

Down

1 - Clothes protectors (4)

2 - Singed (anag) (6)

3 - And 13D:May flowering woodland plant (4,2,3)

4 - Eg bee or wasp (6)

6 - Orange coloured summer annual (8)

9 - The way out (4)

11 - Gardener's friendly annelid (9)

12 - Being perfectly happy (8)

13 - See 3D (6)

15 - Cabbage like vegetable (4)

17 - A long trench (5)

18 - Herb often used with onion (4)

Puzzle 9

Across

1 - ___ tree: small evergreen (6)

7 - Garden tool for pushing (5,3)

8 - Royal Botanical Garden (3)

9 - Candytuft genus (6)

10 - Eg lunch or dinner (4)

11 - Plants with not enough light are this (5)

13 - ___'s Seal: type of lily (7)

15 - An au pair (7)

17 - Female garment (5)

21 - Type of citrus fruit (4)

22 - Covers growing potatoes (6)

23 - Large flightless bird (3)

24 - Egg dish (8)

25 - Mowing tool with long thin blade (6)

Down

1 - Gertrude ___: famous garden designer (6)

2 - Planting seeds (6)

3 - Make attractive (5)

4 - Sound of a sneeze (7)

5 - Plant of Ireland (8)

6 - Edible root (6)

12 - Plants with spike shaped flowers (8)

14 - Under (7)

16 - Eg pea or bean (6)

18 - Six legged creature (6)

19 - Neuter (anag) (6)

20 - Tall substantial plants with a trunk (5)

Puzzle 10

Across

1 - Small furrow in which seed is sown (5)

4 - ___ Flower Show (7)

7 - Garden pest (5)

8 - Delicately (8)

9 - Make ground even (5)

11 - Honeysuckle genus (8)

15 - Prickly small tree with spring blossom (8)

17 - Tacks (5)

19 - A meal in the garden is this (8)

20 - Cut back growth (5)

21 - Small border plant often white (7)

22 - Tree with small black berries (5)

Down

1 - Weed with bright yellow flower (9)

2 - Inhabitants of the sub-continent (7)

3 - Salad vegetable (7)

4 - Less hot (6)

5 - Tool for cutting overhanging branches (6)

6 - A select group (5)

10 - Used to cut the grass (9)

12 - Need mulch to be this? (7)

13 - Rumpled (7)

14 - Striking London trees (6)

16 - Eg garlic or onion (6)

18 - The month of showers! (5)

Puzzle 11

Across

1 - The May tree (8)

5 - Please reply (1,1,1,1)

8 - Spring month (5)

9 - Implements used for cutting and lopping (7)

10 - Loosen soil (7)

12 - Show produce (7)

14 - Person who sells flowers (7)

16 - The highest quality (7)

18 - Hereditary (7)

19 - Heather (5)

20 - Eg ash or elm (4)

21 - Atmospheric conditions (8)

Down

1 - Needed in the greenhouse (4)

2 - Fairly hot (6)

3 - Stinking ___; woodland plant (9)

4 - Fight against (6)

6 - Popular bedding plant; often red (6)

7 - Willow or hazel catkin (5,3)

11 - Portion of public land used for gardening (9)

12 - Faculty of seeing (8)

13 - Used in the bath (6)

14 - Type of grass (6)

15 - Interior part (6)

17 - English trees (4)

Puzzle 12

Across

1 - Evergreen blue flowered plant of the vinca family (10)

6 - Gather in produce (4)

7 - Herb used with pasta (5)

8 - Showy plants with large trumpet shaped flowers (6)

11 - Citrus fruit (5)

12 - Electronic message (1-4)

14 - Light brownish yellow colour (5)

15 - Of the countryside (5)

17 - Run after (5)

19 - Type of movement associated with a horse (6)

21 - Ballroom dance (5)

22 - Pronged garden tool (4)

23 - Evergreen tree important in Australia (10)

Down

1 - Small round stone found on a beach (6)

2 - Colourful plant put in sheltered location (10)

3 - Type of fruit (4)

4 - Rub out (5)

5 - Attractive Spring flowering tree (8)

9 - Make less dark (7)

10 - Black fruit of a small tree (10)

13 - Eg truffle or puffball are types of this (8)

16 - Fragrant Spring flowering shrubs (6)

18 - Aerate the lawn (5)

20 - Smart ___; person with a high self opinion (4)

Puzzle 13

Across

1 - Green vegetable (8)

5 - Familiar form of you (4)

8 - Get together (5)

9 - Framework for climbing plants (7)

10 - Food flavouring from the crocus (7)

12 - Member of the nobility (7)

14 - Samples (7)

16 - Sideboard for displaying dishes etc (7)

18 - Gradual wearing away of the soil (7)

19 - A measuring tool (5)

20 - Very finely powdered earth (4)

21 - Shepherd's best friend (8)

Down

1 - Colour of cornflowers (4)

2 - ___ Twist: Dickens novel (6)

3 - These nuts can be sweet or horse (9)

4 - The most recent (6)

6 - ___ Benn; Minister for the Environment (6)

7 - A sun iris (anag): daisy like flowers (8)

11 - Place away from the freezing cold is this (5,4)

12 - Pernicious weed (8)

13 - Fruits (6)

14 - Deep ditch cut into the ground (6)

15 - Part of the eye (6)

17 - Amphibian found in the pond (4)

Puzzle 14

Across

1 - White springtime flower (8)

5 - Digging implement (4)

7 - Highly scented late spring shrub (5)

8 - Common tree related to the birch (5)

10 - Fast movements by a horse (7)

12 - Green field (7)

14 - Mountain flower eg eidelweiss (6)

16 - Sunshade for the garden (7)

19 - Front tooth (7)

20 - Live or reside (5)

21 - Bow around the waist (4)

22 - Levelling and smoothing the ground (6)

Down

1 - Sodium chloride (4)

2 - Types of primulas (6)

3 - Tree that sheds its leaves (9)

4 - Citrus fruit (6)

6 - Fuel used for the greenhouse maybe (8)

9 - Underground part of a plant (4)

11 - The hedges that grow too quickly! (9)

12 - Vegetables popular at Halloween (8)

13 - Springtime bulb (6)

15 - Inactive (4)

17 - Eg grub or caterpillar (5)

18 - Holly tree (4)

Puzzle 15

Across

1 - Forest tree with grey bark (3)

3 - Bitter aromatic herb (3)

5 - Yellow Spring flowers (abbrev.) (5)

8 - ___ and ends: random objects (4)

9 - Type of plum (8)

11 - Warm building to house tender plants (10)

13 - Plastic tunnel for warming the soil (6)

14 - Study of plants (6)

17 - ___ Brown: landscape gardener (10)

21 - Herb much used in cooking (8)

22 - Smart (4)

23 - Colourful long flowered plant of summer (5)

24 - Tool used to cut wood (3)

25 - Large expanse of water (3)

Down

1 - Surrounded by (5)

2 - Plant divison between fields (8)

4 - Person who runs a newspaper (6)

5 - Fruits grown on palm trees (5)

6 - Land used for agriculture (4)

7 - Loosen and break up soil (7)

10 - Unit of length (4)

12 - Red salad plants (8)

13 - Type of toffee (7)

15 - Leave out (4)

16 - Channels of water (6)

18 - Fruit of the oak (5)

19 - Spiky plant of the agave family (5)

20 - The produce of the garden (4)

Puzzle 16

Across

1 - Do this to the greenhouse in winter (5)

4 - Area for growing speciality plants (7)

7 - Reduce the foliage of plants (5)

8 - Aromatic herb (8)

9 - ___ nut: the nut of the areca palm (5)

11 - Stretch out in length (8)

15 - Common yellow / orange bedding plant (8)

17 - Heather (5)

19 - Very large (8)

20 - Underground swollen parts of perennial plants (5)

21 - Clipping of shrubs into shapes (7)

22 - Female relative (5)

Down

1 - Small vegetable marrow (9)

2 - Soil loss (7)

3 - Tropical cooking spices (7)

4 - Be sorry for (6)

5 - Softer centre of a nut (6)

6 - Series of hills (5)

10 - View of one's garden (9)

12 - Compounds needed in one's diet eg A B or C etc (7)

13 - ___ garden: old fashioned garden (7)

14 - Fish dish usually in breadcrumbs (6)

16 - Place where bees are kept (6)

18 - Abbreviation for rhododendron (5)

Puzzle 17

Across

1 - Summer-house in the garden (6)

3 - Early drooping flower of the willow (6)

7 - Swiss mountain flower (9)

9 - Stick out (8)

10 - Something spoken (4)

12 - Home for an inuit (5)

13 - Tills the land (5)

17 - Track through the garden (4)

18 - 3 leaved plants eg clovers (8)

20 - Prepare soil to the depth of 2 spades (6,3)

21 - British low growing trees with black berries (6)

22 - Tree bearing nuts (6)

Down

1 - Gatherings of people (6)

2 - Deep purple root vegetable (8)

4 - One of the 2 types of soil (4)

5 - Type of weed not wanted in the garden (6)

6 - Root vegetable (5)

7 - Made longer (9)

8 - Cutting grass around the edges (9)

11 - Yellow spring flower (8)

14 - Type of pine tree (6)

15 - Where you sow seeds in the ground (5)

16 - Separate piece of land (6)

19 - Satisfied sound a cat makes (4)

Puzzle 18

Across

1 - Popular interest (9)

7 - Circle of light round a body (4)

9 - Great size (5)

10 - Medicinal or flavoursome plants (5)

11 - Spring shrub (5)

12 - Plantain lily: shade loving perennial (5)

13 - Daisy like flower: rates (anag) (5)

15 - Mild onion flavoured herb (5)

17 - Group in rugby involving the forwards (5)

19 - Layer of grass with earth (4)

20 - A share of land assigned to a person (9)

Down

1 - Plant of the genus muscari flowering in spring (5,8)

2 - Tool with toothed bar used for levelling ground (4)

3 - Attractive young girl named after local flower (7,4)

4 - Tusk of an elephant is made of this (5)

5 - Evergreen hedging shrub (6)

6 - Conker tree (5,8)

8 - A substitute (11)

14 - Eg potatoes (6)

16 - Long thin seed bed (5)

18 - Plant which bears grapes (4)

Puzzle 19

Across

1 - Fragrant Spring flowering plants (11)

9 - Male relative (5)

10 - Type of hedging plant (3)

11 - Cut back in the garden (5)

12 - Succulent plant with fleshy leaves (5)

13 - Fruit tree trained on a lattice (8)

16 - Miniature viola (8)

18 - Enter into a computer (5)

21 - Resident of Middle East state (5)

22 - Pet animal (3)

23 - Imperial measures (5)

24 - Scented climbing plant (11)

Down

2 - Try (7)

3 - Shrubs often used as hedging (7)

4 - To find by searching (6)

5 - Plants in the wrong place (5)

6 - Dressed (5)

7 - Work of outstanding artistry (11)

8 - Test (11)

14 - A work which stands the test of time (7)

15 - Confection of thin layers of rolled up pastry (7)

17 - Candytuft (6)

19 - Outdoor sitting area (5)

20 - Herb (5)

Puzzle 20

Across

1 - Garden transport (11)

7 - Elegant (4)

8 - Tool used with pulling action (5,3)

9 - Layer of eggs (3)

10 - A get together (8)

14 - Friendly garden insect (8)

19 - Type of lettuce (3)

20 - Affecting everything (3-5)

21 - Small pond dwelling amphibian (4)

22 - Red pot plants popular at Christmas (11)

Down

1 - Removing unwanted plants (7)

2 - Soil in which plants grow (5)

3 - Small shrubs (6)

4 - Move further off (6)

5 - Type of tree (4,3)

6 - London ___: street tree (5)

11 - Travel on snow (3)

12 - Root vegetable (7)

13 - Locations where plants grow (7)

15 - Defeated (6)

16 - Tell a story (6)

17 - Fruit of the oak (5)

18 - Mushrooms and toadstools (5)

Puzzle 21

Across

1 - Cuts back plants (6)

3 - Large garden cutting tool (6)

7 - Scented flower of the pink variety (9)

9 - Spring flowering bulbs (8)

10 - Unreturnable serves in tennis (4)

12 - Habitual practice (5)

13 - Type of tea (5)

17 - Citrus fruit (4)

18 - Plant of the genus pelargonium (8)

20 - Common 2 needled coniferous tree (5,4)

21 - Tool that makes a hole in ground (6)

22 - Popular citrus friut (6)

Down

1 - Fencing (6)

2 - Ornaments for the ear (8)

4 - Frozen rain (4)

5 - Vegetable gourd (6)

6 - Small white flower found in grass (5)

7 - And 19D:Winter flower helleborus niger (9,4)

8 - Peach like fruit (9)

11 - Fruit tree trained on a lattice (8)

14 - Nut of the tree prunus dulcis (6)

15 - Raising agent in cooking (5)

16 - Come out (6)

19 - See 7D

Puzzle 22

Across

7 - Shed by trees in the autumn (6)

8 - Tree with lovely spring blossom (6)

10 - Garden refuse used for soil improvement (7)

11 - Tag for identifying plants (5)

12 - Medium to lighten heavy soil (4)

13 - Edible bulb (5)

17 - Cutting strokes made with an axe (5)

18 - Undo (4)

22 - Ballroom dance (5)

23 - Root vegetable (7)

24 - Season for harvesting (6)

25 - Protect plants with this (6)

Down

1 - Sugar occurring in fruit juice (7)

2 - Winter ___: plant bearing yellow flowers (7)

3 - Brush consisting of twigs (5)

4 - Small onion (7)

5 - Crustaceans (5)

6 - Two wheeled transport (5)

9 - Used to bring water to the garden? (9)

14 - Continuously growing underground stem (7)

15 - Popeye's favourite vegetable (7)

16 - Pruned a little bit (7)

19 - Perspire (5)

20 - Roofing medium (5)

21 - Location for sewing seeds (5)

Puzzle 23

Across

1 - Parts of the garden containing large plants (11)

9 - In addition to (5)

10 - Used to row a boat (3)

11 - A shadow (5)

12 - Flavoursome herb (5)

13 - United with someone (8)

16 - ___ rose; floribunda; named after musical piece (8)

18 - ___ seed; loved by garden birds (5)

21 - Sounds made by steam engine (5)

22 - Title of a male teacher (3)

23 - Keep tender plants away from this weather type (5)

24 - Fragrant climbing plant (11)

Down

2 - Vegetation containing perennially flowering plants (7)

3 - Dig up potatoes (7)

4 - ___ brush; cylindrical flowered plant (6)

5 - Means of cooking (5)

6 - Tropical tree with dark heavy wood (5)

7 - Small tree with white flowers and red berries (8,3)

8 - Warm glassed structures for plant protection (11)

14 - Person who doubts the truth of beliefs (7)

15 - Plant having leaves composed of 3 leaflets (7)

17 - Pungent bulbs (6)

19 - Greta ___; 30's film star (5)

20 - Methodical searching of someone else's possessions (

Puzzle 24

Across

1 - Drink made from dried leaves (3)

3 - Soft pear shaped many seeded fruit (3)

5 - A funny person (5)

8 - Ground or soil (4)

9 - Yellow spring flower (8)

11 - Tool used to keep plants in shape (7,3)

13 - Plant with unusual shaped flowers (6)

14 - Spadelike tool (6)

17 - Tasty summer fruit (10)

21 - Fruit tree trained on a lattice (8)

22 - ___ Morecambe: famous comic (4)

23 - Words of a song (5)

24 - To cut grass (3)

25 - Small green vegetable (3)

Down

1 - Spring bulb (5)

2 - Make public (8)

4 - Location to keep the car (6)

5 - Type of butterfly (5)

6 - Heavenly body (4)

7 - Herb with aromatic leaves used for flavouring (7)

10 - ___ fruit: oval fruit with brown skin (4)

12 - Exhaust land by growing too much (8)

13 - Porridge is made from this (7)

15 - Evergreen shrub with flower spikes (4)

16 - Piercing yell (6)

18 - Scented spring shrub (5)

19 - Woody plant of the agave family (5)

20 - Short side shoot (4)

Puzzle 25

Across

1 - Succulent and often spiny plant (6)

7 - Tree - either horse or sweet (8)

8 - Tree with serrated leaves (3)

9 - Basic food vegetable (6)

10 - Tool used for clearing leaves (4)

11 - Low spreading plants can be this (5)

13 - Purple scented spring flowers (7)

15 - Tool used for cutting and pruning (7)

17 - Decorate (5)

21 - Vegetable of the brassica family (4)

22 - Type of lizard (6)

23 - Kernel of an edible seed (3)

24 - Illuminated garden at night is this (8)

25 - A globe or ball shaped object (6)

Down

1 - An angel (6)

2 - University site (6)

3 - Abandoned rubbish (5)

4 - Fleshy plant used for bedding (7)

5 - Surprised (8)

6 - Utensil used to carry water (6)

12 - Closely planted line of bushes (8)

14 - Flavouring obtained from the orchid (7)

16 - Land which can be used for cultivation (6)

18 - Citrus fruit (6)

19 - Stinging weed (6)

20 - Plant diseases caused by fungi (5)

Puzzle 26

Across

1 - Province in the east of Ireland (8)

5 - Purple vegetable (4)

8 - Tree with small purplish black fruit (5)

9 - Strong scented bushy annual (7)

10 - Ivor ___: songwriter (7)

12 - Opened flowers have done this (7)

14 - Fundamental category of plant specification (7)

16 - Absence of rain in the garden (7)

18 - Lasting for ever (7)

19 - Broad and runner are these (5)

20 - Twilight (4)

21 - Fibre used in fireproofing articles: boss seat(anag) (8)

Down

1 - Large vegetable related to the onion (4)

2 - Purplish colour in the rainbow (6)

3 - Cutting the edges of the lawn (9)

4 - Make longer (6)

6 - Praises highly (6)

7 - Dense tufts of grassy vegetation (8)

11 - Food plant (9)

12 - Pernicious weed (8)

13 - Machines used to cut the grass (6)

14 - Leaves are attached to these (6)

15 - Young child (6)

17 - Enquires (4)

Puzzle 27

Across

1 - English fruit (5)

4 - Mowing tools (7)

7 - Fragrant herb (5)

8 - Stoned fruits (8)

9 - Scented spring shrub (5)

11 - Make comments on (8)

15 - Small tree with red fruit (8)

17 - Fruits of the blackthorn (5)

19 - The aubergine (8)

20 - ___ Piper: potato variety (5)

21 - Small onion (7)

22 - Smooth nut of the hickory (5)

Down

1 - Tender vegetable (9)

2 - Raining heavily (7)

3 - Impart knowledge (7)

4 - Group of 6 (6)

5 - Very disastrous (6)

6 - Heath shrub (5)

10 - Flower suitable for buttonhole (9)

12 - A temporary substitute (7)

13 - Relating to plants (7)

14 - Antenna (6)

16 - Summer month (6)

18 - Dog lead (5)

Puzzle 28

Across

1 - Type of cabbage (5)

4 - Squash used at Halloween (7)

7 - Aromatic herb (5)

8 - Bee - keeper (8)

9 - Fragrant spring shrub (5)

11 - Plant with white juice: mild week (anag) (8)

15 - Plant grown flat against a wall (8)

17 - Aromatic bitter herb with yellow button flowers (5)

19 - The common honeysuckle (8)

20 - Aquatic mammal (5)

21 - An axe used for wood cutting (7)

22 - Root vegetable (5)

Down

1 - Type of garden flavouring plant (9)

2 - Fragrant pod of the orchid used to flavour (7)

3 - Perennial wild flowers good in borders (7)

4 - Chase (6)

5 - Very calm (6)

6 - One of the Balearic islands (5)

10 - Small vegetable marrow (9)

12 - Places where we practise horticulture (7)

13 - Can be seen (7)

14 - Not awake (6)

16 - Small amount of rain (6)

18 - One of the letters of the alphabet (5)

Puzzle 29

Across

1 - Weeding tool used by pushing (5-3)

5 - A film heroic in scale (4)

8 - Reduce cuttings to small pieces (5)

9 - Vegetable of the brassica family (7)

10 - Not outdoors (7)

12 - Matured produce has done this (7)

14 - A baby frog (7)

16 - Alfresco (4-3)

18 - Make stronger (7)

19 - Part of a dartboard next to the bull (5)

20 - Classic summer flower (4)

21 - Heavy rainy and humid weather (8)

Down

1 - Twilight (4)

2 - Staple vegetable (6)

3 - Showy shrub: garden hay (anag) (9)

4 - Exotic looking flower eg lady's slipper (6)

6 - Seed case containing vegetables (3,3)

7 - Oily liquid used for fence preservation (8)

11 - Common yellow weed (9)

12 - Person who writes for a newspaper (8)

13 - Perennial fleshy plants: mussed (anag) (6)

14 - Dig this to sow seeds in (6)

15 - Citrus fruit (6)

17 - Drab colour (4)

Puzzle 30

Across

1 - Red fruit used in salads (6)

3 - Tasty small red fruit grown on trees (6)

7 - Yellow Spring flowering shrub (9)

9 - Many herbs have this quality (8)

10 - As well as (4)

12 - Yellow citrus fruit (5)

13 - Great (5)

17 - Dig up vegetables eg potatoes (4)

18 - Large red sweet peppers (8)

20 - Implement used to cut the grass (4,5)

21 - Vitality (6)

22 - Perennial herb with camphor like smell (6)

Down

1 - Front part of the neck (6)

2 - Herb whose leaves flavour salads and soups (8)

4 - Ditch forming garden boundary (2-2)

5 - Colour of a primrose (6)

6 - Words of a tune (5)

7 - Having many blooms - ruffle owl (anag) (9)

8 - Animal like a crocodile (9)

11 - Eg a canal or ditch (8)

14 - Sheep's coat (6)

15 - Popular holiday destination in Florida (5)

16 - Not awake (6)

19 - Small branch (4)

Puzzle 31

Across

7 - Protection for tender plants (6)

8 - Herb with strong scent of aniseed (6)

10 - Spring flowering plant - genus includes cowslip (7)

11 - What the Zephirine Drouhin rose does not have (5)

12 - Tall slender leaved plant of the grass family (4)

13 - Even (5)

17 - Coldly (5)

18 - Large yellowy dessert fruit (4)

22 - Plant with thorny stem eg blackberry (5)

23 - ___ violet: small house plant (7)

24 - Sea ___: flower suitable for rock gardens (6)

25 - John ___: Beatle (6)

Down

1 - Royal ceremonial staff (7)

2 - Mainly evergreen tree (7)

3 - Woody plant of low height (5)

4 - Low growing shrub with pinkish flowers (7)

5 - Pungent bulb used in cooking (5)

6 - London ___: tall hardy tree (5)

9 - Evergreen shrubs of the tea family (9)

14 - Aerate the ground (7)

15 - Barrier around the garden (7)

16 - Reducing the growth of a plant (7)

19 - Water holder (1,4)

20 - Metric unit of volume (5)

21 - What all environmentalists are? (5)

Puzzle 32

Across

7 - Large clipping tool (6)

8 - Pungent bulb used in cooking (6)

10 - Distant line where earth and sky meet (7)

11 - Type of orange (5)

12 - Series of names (4)

13 - Grass lawn (5)

17 - Note daily garden events in this (5)

18 - Measure of weight (abbrev) (4)

22 - Spring flowering purple or white shrub (5)

23 - ___ fruit: many seeded fruit (7)

24 - Flower of the willow or hazel (6)

25 - Cuts back foliage (6)

Down

1 - Suitable path covering? (7)

2 - Hybrid thornless plant - usually yellowish / pink (3,4)

3 - A winner usually receives this (5)

4 - Harvests: rangers (anag) (7)

5 - Mediterranean tree (5)

6 - Range of values used for measuring (5)

9 - White early springtime flowers (9)

14 - Goes well with a cup of tea! (7)

15 - Mental images (7)

16 - Lost Gardens of Heligan is a ___ garden (7)

19 - Material used for paving or building (5)

20 - Allotment sites (5)

21 - Russian rulers (5)

Puzzle 33

Across

1 - Tool used to make a hole for bulb planting (6)

4 - Type of plum (6)

9 - Popular flowering annual used in hanging baskets (7)

10 - Sound made by lightning (7)

11 - Metric heavy weight (5)

12 - Refresh (5)

14 - London ___: perennial garden plant (5)

15 - Daisy like flower typically purple or pink (5)

17 - Outdoor area suitable for pot plants (5)

18 - Need these type of plants for your pond (7)

20 - Exotic fruit difficult to grow here (7)

21 - Loosen the soil with a fork (6)

22 - Pungent herb for cooking (6)

Down

1 - A substitute in position of authority (6)

2 - Person who studies plants (8)

3 - Premium Bond generator (1,1,1,1,1)

5 - Come into possession of (7)

6 - Garden den for storing implements (4)

7 - Not wide (6)

8 - Tool used to pour liquid (8-3)

13 - To do with the sea (8)

14 - The function of a cloche (7)

15 - Rhododendron like shrub (6)

16 - Verse like writing (6)

17 - ___ ham: food delicacy (5)

19 - An enjoyer of a facility (4)

Puzzle 34

Across

7 - These grow on trees (6)

8 - Feathery leaved herb used with fish (6)

10 - Genus of the lilac (7)

11 - This will grow on most roses (5)

12 - A citrus fruit hybrid (4)

13 - Tool used to tidy verges (5)

17 - You see this in the garden (5)

18 - Currency in France and Spain (4)

22 - You raise this over growing potatoes (5)

23 - Ebbs away (7)

24 - Tool used to remove unwanted plants (6)

25 - Aids needed to support growing plants (6)

Down

1 - Small flowering spring plant usually white or yellow (7)

2 - Trees used for emblems of victory (7)

3 - Large variously coloured flower: y open (anag) (5)

4 - Moorland plant normally purple (7)

5 - Pungent bulb (5)

6 - London ___: type of tree (5)

9 - What all our readers are! (9)

14 - Sheepskins which keep us warm (7)

15 - Weedy biennial plant that goes well with dandelion (7)

16 - Own (7)

19 - Colour of the earth (5)

20 - Unwanted snake in the garden (5)

21 - Very sharp (5)

Puzzle 35

Across

1 - Showy plant with tuberous roots:ah dial (anag) (6)

7 - Climbing plant (8)

8 - English deciduous tree (3)

9 - Type of squash with green skin (6)

10 - Cabbage like vegetable (4)

11 - Word of regret (5)

13 - Mixed organic manure (7)

15 - Types of plums (7)

17 - Small leaved plant with edible leaves (5)

21 - Gardener's friend in aerating the soil (4)

22 - Red salad vegetable (6)

23 - What peas come in (3)

24 - Get larger in size (8)

25 - Grows or elevates (6)

Down

1 - Imagines (6)

2 - Tool used for driving nails (6)

3 - Maple trees (5)

4 - US native tree eg sequoia (7)

5 - Annual flower of the delphinium genus (8)

6 - Small pansies (6)

12 - Herb used particularly with lamb (8)

14 - First or beginning (7)

16 - Seeds of the oaks (6)

18 - Runs away with (6)

19 - Tools used for digging (6)

20 - Red brown earthy colour (5)

Across

1 - Type of fruit tree (5,6)

9 - Insect larva: semi divine spirit (5)

10 - Level score at golf (3)

11 - Turnips or swedes (Scottish dialect) (5)

12 - Frogs' eggs found in garden pond (5)

13 - Large purple skinned fruit (8)

16 - Common garden blackish-brown bird (8)

18 - Make a member of a club (5)

21 - Sweet orange-fleshed tropical fruit (5)

22 - Kernel of a hard shelled fruit (3)

23 - Ancient king with the golden touch (5)

24 - Small deciduous tree with bright orange berries (8,3)

Down

2 - Ancestry or pedigree (7)

3 - Comfort in distress (7)

4 - Large area of open land (6)

5 - Characteristic nature of a community (5)

6 - Society which cares for animals (1,1,1,1,1)

7 - Popular garden vegetable grown on a frame (6,5)

8 - Garden tool with a long pole and curved blade (7,4)

14 - Deep red colour of some geraniums (7)

15 - Little fish in a stream (7)

17 - Vast treeless Arctic region (6)

19 - Relationship between 2 quantities (5)

20 - Citrus fruit (5)

Puzzle 37

Across

1 - Fruit of the blackthorn (4)

3 - Keeping the garden green by this means (8)

9 - Green with vegetation (7)

10 - Headgear worn by a queen (5)

11 - Communicate in the Alps (5)

12 - ___ and tenon: type of joint on garden shed (7)

13 - A planting of bulbs maybe (1,5)

15 - Boggy ground (6)

17 - Part of one's house (7)

18 - Children's charity which often benefits from garden viewings (1,1,1,1,1)

20 - Group of trees (5)

21 - Brilliant blue alpine flower: antigen (anag) (7)

22 - Evasive move in rugby (8)

23 - A garden pergola (4)

Down

1 - Varieties of brassicas (5,8)

2 - Rowed (5)

4 - Time for planting Spring bulbs (6)

5 - Showing outdoor hospitality to garden guests (12)

6 - Type of font (7)

7 - Plant of the genus muscari (5,8)

8 - Vegetables which require a fertile soil (12)

14 - Type of tropical tree (7)

16 - A political exile (6)

19 - Beforehand (5)

38

Puzzle 38

Across

1 - A shower or precipitation welcome for garden (8)

5 - A plant stalk (4)

7 - Japanese sport of fencing (5)

8 - Starts potatoes sprouting (5)

10 - The most important element of something (7)

12 - A V-shaped badge on a uniform sleeve (7)

14 - Aromatic herb of the mint family (6)

16 - Plantation of conifers (7)

19 - Herb of the parsley family with small white flowers (7)

20 - A magazine copy (5)

21 - Soil debris on the bottom of a garden pond (4)

22 - Roof covering made with reeds (6)

Down

1 - Garden tool with a toothed bar (4)

2 - Set fire to an object (6)

3 - Plant container (9)

4 - Greeny/grey organism that grows on plants (6)

6 - Tree grown for its purple fruit (8)

9 - Granular material used to lighten heavy soil (4)

11 - Very aromatic culinary herb (9)

12 - Cuts down trees periodically (8)

13 - Feeling ill (6)

15 - Lubricates (4)

17 - Mixture of wet leaves spread round plant roots (5)

18 - Pungent vegetable (4)

Puzzle 39

Across

1 - Plant seeds (3)

3 - Gardener's refuge and storage location (3)

5 - A shortish woody plant (5)

8 - Decays (4)

9 - Useful garden aids when planting out (8)

11 - Type of summer fruit (10)

13 - Edible apple shaped fruit (6)

14 - Capital of Greece (6)

17 - Tools for cutting the grass (10)

21 - Hero of an epic poem by Homer (8)

22 - Mercian king who has a dyke named after him (4)

23 - A farm animal (5)

24 - A high shot in tennis (3)

25 - Person who is clever with their remarks (3)

Down

1 - Vegetation consisting of stunted trees and shrubs (5)

2 - Areas of poor soil drainage (8)

4 - Grow tender plants in here (6)

5 - Cut the wool from sheep (5)

6 - Tall broad-leaved grass that grows in water (4)

7 - Useful containers for flowers and plants (7)

10 - Plant also known as lady's fingers (4)

12 - Aromatic white herb used to treat migraine (8)

13 - Herbaceous plants with pink or purple flowers: sallmow (anag) (7)

15 - Something which is an aid (4)

16 - A plant which grows for 1 year only (6)

18 - Author of Fables (5)

19 - The slope of a piece of ground (5)

20 - A unit of data of 8 binary digits (4)

Puzzle 40

Across

1 - Spring flowering bulb (6)

7 - Jewellery (8)

8 - Viscous liquid obtainable from eg linseed (3)

9 - A colour of the rainbow (6)

10 - Arrange to get together with a friend (4)

11 - SE English county (5)

13 - Protection from birds for plants (7)

15 - An autumn vegetable of the gourd family (7)

17 - Tall fast growing tree of the willow family (5)

21 - To do with the mouth (4)

22 - Type of potato (6)

23 - Necessary object for housing a plant (3)

24 - Salad of raw cabbage and mayonnaise (8)

25 - Seat used for riding on a horse (6)

Down

1 - Garden protection for tender plants in winter (6)

2 - Hybrids of primroses (6)

3 - Garden pest (5)

4 - The month to create a new vegetable patch and harvest carrots and apples (7)

5 - Very popular climbing garden plant (8)

6 - Device to separate out various sections of the garden (6)

12 - Fruit tree or shrub whose branches are trained to grow flat against a wall (8)

14 - Annual flower often known as love in a mist (7)

16 - To dig up a plant (6)

18 - The husk or outer casing of edible vegetable seeds (3,3)

19 - An unwanted stinging plant (6)

20 - A dish of meat and vegetables cooked slowly in liquid in a closed dish (5)

Puzzle 41

Across

1 - Early spring flowering bulb (8)

5 - Soft pear shaped fruits (4)

8 - What a climbing plant does (5)

9 - Winter ___: yellow flowered small spring plant (7)

10 - A sepal: small sheet of printed matter (7)

12 - A communication (7)

14 - A fragrant plant of the iris family: see fair (anag) (7)

16 - Brightly coloured S African plant: main see (anag) (7)

18 - Heavy tools to flatten the ground (7)

19 - The sub-continent (5)

20 - Means of removing water from the ground (4)

21 - A sporting activity on the sea (5,3)

Down

1 - Receptacle for potatoes or other root vegetables (4)

2 - Pungent bulbs (6)

3 - The foxglove (9)

4 - A foreteller of the future (6)

6 - Frozen hanging water (6)

7 - Very fragrant climbing flower (5,3)

11 - The egg plant (9)

12 - Vegetables gathered in the prevailing season (4,4)

13 - A symbol (6)

14 - A small tree of the ginseng family: if a sat(anag) (6)

15 - Digging tools (6)

17 - A cab (4)

Puzzle 42

Across

1 - Colourful spring bulb (8)

6 - Repeat the sound (4)

8 - Device used to protect plants (6)

9 - A plant turns this when kept in damp conditions (6)

10 - Indication of maiden name (3)

11 - A gemstone noted for its rich iridescence (4)

12 - Small insectivorous bog plant (6)

13 - Fencing around a plot (6)

15 - An expensive product (6)

17 - Put in safe-keeping (6)

20 - Another name for the mountain lion (4)

21 - Bitter aromatic herb (3)

22 - Ground covering used to warm or protect plants (6)

23 - Currency of Russia (6)

24 - An inhabitant of Bangkok (4)

25 - A bush named in a nursery rhyme (8)

Down

2 - A leaf on the pond (4-3)

3 - Do very well at something (5)

4 - ___ primrose: 4 petalled yellow flower (7)

5 - Green fruits (5)

6 - The time when the day and night are of equal length (7)

7 - A barrier made of plants (5)

14 - An inhabitant of Tel Aviv (7)

15 - Relating to sideways movement (7)

16 - Type of rose (7)

18 - A fine earth (5)

19 - Imagine (5)

20 - To cut back a plant or tree (5)

Puzzle 43

Across

1 - A specialist cook (4)

3 - Sweet sounds of birds in the Spring (8)

9 - Burrowing animals that can devastate crops (7)

10 - Last letter of the Greek alphabet (5)

11 - To plant seeds (3)

12 - Shaped like an egg (5)

15 - A dog like carnivore (5)

16 - A pouchlike structure in a plant or an animal (3)

17 - Material used for strong fence posts (5)

18 - Highest mountain in Wales (7)

19 - A pillar which commemorates the Great Fire of London (8)

20 - Netting to keep plants free from pests (4)

Down

1 - Colourful autumn flower: national flower of Japan (13)

2 - Joint in the arm (5)

4 - Aromatic bitter tasting herb with small blue flowers (6)

5 - Spring flowering evergreen shrub akin to azalea (12)

6 - Nordic country (7)

7 - Spring bulb of the muscari family (5,8)

8 - Popular variety of a fruit tree (8,4)

13 - A football club from Liverpool (7)

14 - Small dark type of plum (6)

16 - Narrow leaved marshy plant (5)

Puzzle 44

Across

1 - Choose the strongest plant (6)

5 - Female swan (3)

7 - Separate out stones from the compost (5)

8 - Type of onion (7)

9 - ___ snap peas: vegetable (5)

10 - Long green fleshy salad fruit (8)

12 - Scupture adorning the garden? (6)

14 - Plant whose root is used in Japanese cookery (6)

17 - ___ can: tool used to keep plants from drying out (8)

18 - Damp (5)

20 - Mixed manure of organic origin (7)

21 - ___ daisy: attractive wild flower (2-3)

22 - Industrious communal insect (3)

23 - Type of plant eg petunia and sweet pea (6)

Down

2 - Part of a car: tire out (7)

3 - Discoverer of America (8)

4 - Busy social insects that fertilise plants (4)

5 - Attractive arched framework used for climbing plants (7)

6 - Capital of Kenya (7)

7 - The act of soaking seeds before planting (5)

11 - A representative (8)

12 - Small evergreen shrub with red berries (7)

13 - Orange fruit best grown fan trained against a wall (7)

15 - Australian evergreen shrub: ask bani (anag) (7)

16 - Eg tabasco or Worcester (5)

19 - Attaches a plant to a stake (4)

Puzzle 45

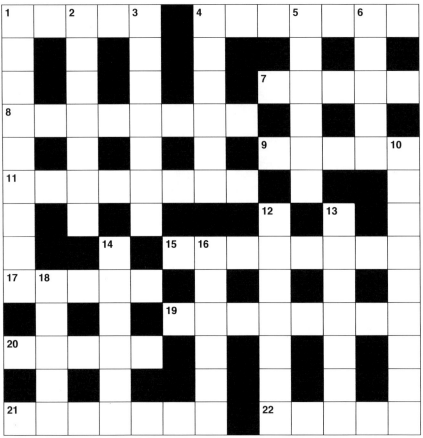

Across

1 - Eg Maris Pipers or Charlottes (colloq) (5)

4 - Spread damp leaves etc round plant roots (7)

7 - Perform a yearly task in the greenhouse (5)

8 - A herbaceous plant with bold flower spikes: cash aunt (anag) (8)

9 - ___'s ladder: favourite plant for shade with clusters of blue flowers (5)

11 - The manager of a resting place for travellers (8)

15 - System to remove excess water from ground (8)

17 - Flower associated with Holland (5)

19 - Tall perennial plant of the genus digitalis (8)

20 - Aromatic seeds of a plant of the parsley family used as a spice in curry powder. (5)

21 - Brian ___: English actor with a sonorous voice (7)

22 - Plant used as a herb with buttonlike yellow flower heads (5)

Down

1 - Fragrant variety of well used herb (9)

2 - Find something in the ground (7)

3 - Town in US state of Washington: home of Frasier (7)

4 - Compost spread on ground to fertilize it (6)

5 - Use this to avoid cabbage root fly? (6)

6 - The Greek muse of poetry (5)

10 - A fruit of a dwarf shrub with whitish flowers (9)

12 - A butterfly: girl net (anag) (7)

13 - A fatty substance found naturally on sheep's wool (7)

14 - Peruvian ___: alstroemeria flowers (6)

16 - A plant which has started to grow is this (6)

18 - Ordinarily practised (5)

Puzzle 46

Across

1 - Cold dishes of raw green vegetables (6)

3 - Tool used for cutting back branches (6)

7 - Collections of cabbages sprouts and kale etc (9)

9 - Low growing weed (8)

10 - A maple or sycamore tree (4)

12 - Vegetation which mainly consists of stunted shrubs and trees (5)

13 - Large evergreen trees with a crown of leaves (5)

17 - Showy flower with name meaning rainbow (4)

18 - ___ Da Vinci: famous artist (8)

20 - Popular tall flower with sword shaped leaves (9)

21 - A gourd (6)

22 - The bay tree (6)

Down

1 - Remains of trees that have been cut down (6)

2 - A flower of the pink family (8)

4 - Staple food in the East (4)

5 - Relay a lawn (6)

6 - Seaport of Ancient Rome (5)

7 - How trees spread by dividing (9)

8 - Trees with winged seeds (9)

11 - Tree cultivated for the Spring with showy flowers (8)

14 - Type of fruit eg lemon or orange (6)

15 - ___ Smith: celebrity cook (5)

16 - Herbal plant sometimes used in salads (6)

19 - Fruits of the may tree (4)

Puzzle 47

Across

1 - Herb used with onion in stuffing (4)

3 - Type of rose (8)

9 - ___ up: covered growing potato plants (7)

10 - Tree common in wet places (5)

11 - Not here (5)

12 - Troublesome (7)

13 - Drink in (6)

15 - Type of eating apple (6)

17 - Yellow toadflax belongs to this genus: air nail (anag) (7)

18 - Early summer flowering plant (abbrev) (5)

20 - ___ acids: compounds that are building blocks of proteins (5)

21 - A stannary (3-4)

22 - Person who is knowledgeable about plants (8)

23 - Mushrooms (4)

Down

1 - Biennial plants (5,8)

2 - A yellow flowered shrub (5)

4 - Buzz ___: 2nd man on the moon (6)

5 - Dark small fruit (12)

6 - Opposite of alfresco (7)

7 - Tools used for lifting plants (6-7)

8 - Equipment used to transport garden material (12)

14 - A conflagration to remove unwanted matter (7)

16 - The sister of Mary in the Bible (6)

19 - Small fruit used to make oil (5)

Puzzle 48

Across

1 - Antirrhinum (10)

6 - Watercress is rich in this element (4)

7 - A French goodbye (5)

8 - ___ McDowell or ___ Swann (6)

11 - One was fired by William Tell (5)

12 - One of the Balearic Islands (5)

14 - A cold dish of vegetables such as lettuce or cucumber (5)

15 - Common British low growing tree with small black berries (5)

17 - ___ Lama: Tibetan Buddhist leader (5)

19 - Part of a tree (6)

21 - Round fruit picked in the autumn (5)

22 - Capital of Norway (4)

23 - Member of the genus Ribes (10)

Down

1 - Type of langoustine (6)

2 - An evergreen conifer (7-3)

3 - Richard ___: US film star (4)

4 - These seeds are loved by birds (5)

5 - A heated glass building for growing plants (8)

9 - Relating to the region of Norfolk and Suffolk (7)

10 - Popular type of fern (10)

13 - A person who studies plants (8)

16 - Eg the mouse that gnaws potatoes is this (6)

18 - Strongly dislike (5)

20 - Type of soil suitable for camellias and heathers (4)

Puzzle 49

Across

1 - Evergreen tree (5,3)

5 - Cuckoo ___: evidence of garden pest (4)

8 - Herb of the allium family (5)

9 - Citrus fruit (7)

10 - Large destructive beetles (7)

12 - Type of bean (7)

14 - Tool with keener cutting edge is this (7)

16 - Type of pepper (7)

18 - Plants that sting (7)

19 - An attractive perennial with long flower (5)

20 - Garden tools (4)

21 - Plant beneath other plants (8)

Down

1 - Container to store potatoes (4)

2 - Jamie ___: TV cook (6)

3 - Vegetable with tassels (9)

4 - Eg bee or wasp (6)

6 - Reduced growth on plant (6)

7 - Move from 1 area to another (8)

11 - Broad bean variety for winter sowing (9)

12 - Bulb grown for Christmas display (8)

13 - Evergreen sweet scented shrub: try elm (anag) (6)

14 - Eg winter or summer (6)

15 - ___ grass: decorative garden feature (6)

17 - Winter weather feature (4)

Across

1 - Plant grown for its edible pungent root (11)

9 - Classic garden flowers (5)

10 - Small round green seed (3)

11 - ---- Federer: tennis champion (5)

12 - A body with no space inside (5)

13 - A score less one (8)

16 - Little cucumbers used for pickling (8)

18 - Insect larva found in garden ponds (5)

21 - Bone in the lower leg (5)

22 - To possess an object (3)

23 - A genus of shrubs including berries (5)

24 - Common blue summer plants (11)

Down

2 - A herb related to marjoram (7)

3 - A leaf with notched edges (7)

4 - To save a situation (6)

5 - Dry particles of earth (5)

6 - Green part of a flower enclosing the petals (5)

7 - Plant of the allium family (6,5)

8 - Tool for digging (6,5)

14 - Tool for cutting shapes in wood (7)

15 - Garden implement for making holes in the ground (7)

17 - To do with plants associated with flavouring (6)

19 - Oval yellowish tropical fruit (5)

20 - One needs to protect garden pond against this bird (5)

Puzzle 51

Across

7 - Tool used to cut back shrubs (6)

8 - ___ potato: type of early potato (6)

10 - Portion of a game in cricket (7)

11 - ___ daisy: grassland flower (2-3)

12 - Engrave on metal or glass by means of a protective layer (4)

13 - A tree of the willow family (5)

17 - The country from which knot weed comes (5)

18 - Prickly seed head of a plant (4)

22 - Type of Indian tea (5)

23 - Radioactive chemical element (7)

24 - Characteristic of a cat (6)

25 - Cold temperate region dominated by forests of birch and poplars etc (6)

Down

1 - Small plants that like mountainous conditions (7)

2 - Green vegetable (7)

3 - Showy flower (5)

4 - Colourful flower with bright foliage: I ban ego (anag) (7)

5 - European poplar tree (5)

6 - Part of a plant that conducts water and nutrients: ley mx (anag) (5)

9 - Vegetable eaten in the Spring as a delicacy (9)

14 - Winter ___: plant with yellow flowers (7)

15 - Evergreen tree with bluish black berries (7)

16 - A blackberry bush (7)

19 - Type of orange (5)

20 - A sacred song (5)

21 - Type of cabbage (5)

Puzzle 52

Across

1 - Turn the ground with a spade (3)

3 - Variety of lettuce (3)

5 - Tool used to remove grit from soil (5)

8 - Layer of grass and earth (4)

9 - Perennial summer flowering herb with sweetly scented flowers (8)

11 - A sweet tasting summer fruit (10)

13 - One of the colours of the rainbow (6)

14 - A soft and light protective layer that can be placed over plants (6)

17 - Popular garden plant of the buttercup family with tall spikes of blue flowers: upheld mini (anag) (10)

21 - Tropical tree with hard reddish-brown timber (8)

22 - The action of taking a cutting (4)

23 - Ravi Shankar played this stringed instrument (5)

24 - Fluid or juice that circulates in a plant (3)

25 - Bitter aromatic herb (3)

Down

1 - Fruits of the palm tree (5)

2 - ___ Jekyll: famous horticulturist of the last century (8)

4 - Drenched in water (6)

5 - To cut or clip vegetation (5)

6 - ___ Robson: co-host of Gardeners' Question Time (4)

7 - Raise to the peerage (7)

10 - Stick like part of a tree (4)

12 - Eg Capability Brown was this: a garden ___ (8)

13 - Narrow portion of land enclosed by water (7)

15 - ___ Lane: Superman's girlfriend (4)

16 - These cover a cactus (6)

18 - Tool used for creating straight lines round a lawn (5)

19 - An acer (5)

20 - To allow potatoes to sprout eyes (4)

Puzzle 53

Across

7 - Tool like a spade to move earth (6)

8 - Seeding (6)

10 - Of the moment (7)

11 - ___ trees are a feature of London (5)

12 - Where the sun rises (4)

13 - ___ grass; the dreaded pest (5)

17 - Sweet smelling culinary herb (5)

18 - Cut off the top of a tree (4)

22 - The centre (5)

23 - Meanies (anag) (7)

24 - Where the RHS is based (6)

25 - Acceptance of a doctrine (6)

Down

1 - Forest dweller with grey bark (3,4)

2 - Mixed manure from garden waste (7)

3 - Nut bearing tree (5)

4 - Compress (7)

5 - Sweetly scented spring shrub syringa (5)

6 - Small white heron (5)

9 - Grow one's own food here (9)

14 - Pungent condiment (7)

15 - Upper layer of the garden plot (7)

16 - Violet flowered fodder plant (7)

19 - Displays (5)

20 - Attractive annuals of the viola family (5)

21 - Yellow resin (5)

Puzzle 1

R	O	S	E	S	■	■	F	U	C	H	S	I	A
A	■	T	■	K	■	E	■	■	E	■	R	■	■
S	■	R	■	E	■	N	■	F	R	U	I	T	■
P	L	A	N	T	I	N	G	■	B	■	S	■	■
B	■	N	■	C	■	E	■	M	A	T	H	S	■
E	G	G	S	H	E	L	L	■	L	■	■	E	■
R	■	E	■	Y	■	■	■	T	■	O	■	C	■
R	■	■	A	■	A	M	P	H	I	B	I	A	■
Y	O	U	N	G	■	A	■	I	■	V	■	T	■
■	A	N	■	S	U	N	S	H	I	N	E	■	■
I	S	S	U	E	■	V	■	T	■	O	■	U	■
■	I	A	■	■	■	E	■	L	■	U	■	R	■
U	S	E	L	E	S	S	■	E	A	S	E	S	■

Puzzle 2

L	A	B	U	R	N	U	M	■	W	E	E	D
O	A	U	■	L	■	■	A	■	R
V	M	N	■	S	■	F	U	R	Z	E
A	B	N	A	T	A	L	■	T	■	D
G	L	O	B	E	■	E	■	O	■	H	■	G
E	O	R	■	R	■	R	O	S	I	E
■	B	■	■	I	■	■	■
S	P	A	D	E	■	C	■	B	■	A	■	C
H	Z	A	■	E	■	U	N	D	E	R
O	A	N	Y	L	O	N	■	V	■	O
V	O	L	E	S	■	E	■	D	■	N	■	U
E	E	■	■	R	■	A	■	N	■	U
L	E	A	F	■	M	Y	O	S	O	T	I	S

Puzzle 3

Puzzle 4

Puzzle 5

Puzzle 6

Puzzle 7

Puzzle 8

Puzzle 9

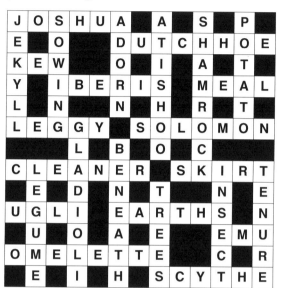

```
J O S H U A ■ A ■ S ■ P ■
E ■ O ■ ■ D U T C H H O E
K E W ■ O ■ I ■ A ■ T ■
Y ■ I B E R I S ■ M E A L
■ L N ■ N ■ H ■ R ■ T ■
L E G G Y ■ ■ S O L O M O N
■ ■ L ■ B ■ O ■ C ■
C L E A N E R ■ S K I R T
■ E ■ D ■ N ■ T ■ N ■ E
U G L I ■ E A R T H S ■ N
■ U ■ O ■ A ■ E ■ ■ E M U
O M E L E T T E ■ ■ C ■ R
■ E ■ I ■ H ■ S C Y T H E
```

Puzzle 10

```
D R I L L ■ C H E L S E A
A ■ N ■ E ■ O ■ ■ O ■ L ■
N ■ D ■ T ■ O ■ A P H I D
D A I N T I L Y ■ P ■ T ■
E ■ A ■ U ■ E ■ L E V E L
L O N I C E R A ■ R ■ ■ A
I ■ S ■ E ■ ■ S ■ T ■ W
O ■ ■ P ■ H A W T H O R N
N A I L S ■ L ■ E ■ U ■ M
■ P ■ A ■ A L F R E S C O
P R U N E ■ I ■ I ■ L ■ W
■ I ■ E ■ ■ U ■ L ■ E ■ E
A L Y S S U M ■ E L D E R
```

Puzzle 11

```
H A W T H O R N ■ R S V P
E ■ A ■ E ■ E ■ ■ A ■ U
A P R I L ■ S I C K L E S
T ■ M ■ L ■ I ■ V ■ S
■ T ■ E ■ S C A R I F Y
E X H I B I T ■ L ■ A ■ C
Y ■ ■ O ■ ■ L ■ L ■ A
■ E ■ S ■ R ■ F L O R I S T
S U P R E M E ■ T ■ N
I ■ O ■ ■ S ■ M ■ S ■ O
G E N E T I C ■ E R I C A
H ■ G ■ ■ U ■ N ■ D ■ K
T R E E ■ W E A T H E R S
```

Puzzle 12

```
P E R I W I N K L E ■ M ■
E ■ ■ A ■ ■ I ■ R E A P
B A S I L ■ ■ W ■ A ■ G
B ■ ■ L I L I E S ■ G
L ■ F ■ I ■ L E M O N
E M A I L ■ G ■ D ■ L
■ U ■ O C H R E ■ ■ I
■ S ■ W ■ T ■ R U R A L
C H A S E ■ E ■ B ■ ■ I
■ R ■ P R A N C E ■ ■ L
O ■ I ■ L ■ R U M B A
F O R K ■ E ■ R ■ ■ C
■ M ■ E U C A L Y P T U S
```

Puzzle 13

B	R	O	C	C	O	L	I			T	H	O	U	
L		L		H		A				I		R		
U	N	I	T	E		T	R	E	L	L	I	S		
E		V		S		E			A		I			
		E		T		S	A	F	F	R	O	N		
B	A	R	O	N	E	T		R		Y		I		
I			U				R		O			A		
N		M		T		T	A	S	T	E	R	S		
D	R	E	S	S	E	R		T		Y				
W		L				E		F		E		F		
E	R	O	S	I	O	N		R	U	L	E	R		
E		N				C		E		I		O		
D	U	S	T		S	H	E	E	P	D	O	G		

Puzzle 14

S	N	O	W	D	R	O	P			F	O	R	K	
A		X		E		R						E		
L	I	L	A	C		A	L	D	E	R		R		
T		I		I		N			O			O		
		P		D		G	A	L	L	O	P	S		
P	A	S	T	U	R	E		E		T		E		
U			O			Y		Y				N		
M		C	U			A	L	P	I	N	E			
P	A	R	A	S	O	L		A		D				
K		O		A		N		N		L		I		
I	N	C	I	S	O	R		D	W	E	L	L		
N		U		V		I		I				E		
S	A	S	H		R	A	K	I	N	G		X		

Puzzle 15

A	S	H		R	U	E		D	A	F	F	S
M		E			D		A		A			C
O	D	D	S		V	I	C	T	O	R	I	A
N		G		I		T		E		M		R
G	R	E	E	N	H	O	U	S	E			I
		R		C		R			R			F
C	L	O	C	H	E		B	O	T	A	N	Y
A		W			C		M		D			
R			C	A	P	A	B	I	L	I	T	Y
A		C		C		N		T		S		U
M	A	R	J	O	R	A	M		C	H	I	C
E		O		R		L				E		C
L	U	P	I	N		S	A	W		S	E	A

Puzzle 16

C	L	E	A	N		R	O	C	K	E	R	Y
O		R		U		E			E		A	
U		O		T		G		P	R	U	N	E
R	O	S	E	M	A	R	Y		N		G	
G		I		E		E		B	E	T	E	L
E	L	O	N	G	A	T	E		L			A
T		N		S		V		C				N
T			S		M	A	R	I	G	O	L	D
E	R	I	C	A		P		T		T		S
	H		A		G	I	G	A	N	T	I	C
C	O	R	M	S		A		M		A		A
	D		P		R		I		G		P
T	O	P	I	A	R	Y		N	I	E	C	E

Puzzle 17

```
G A Z E B O ■ C A T K I N ■
R ■ ■ ■ E ■ S ■ C ■ ■ ■ ■ E
O ■ E D E L W E I S S ■ ■ T
U ■ L ■ T ■ E ■ D ■ T ■ T ■
P R O T R U D E ■ O R A L ■
S ■ N ■ O ■ E ■ D ■ I ■ E ■
■ I G L O O ■ F A R M S ■ ■
S ■ A ■ T ■ D ■ F ■ M ■ I ■
P A T H ■ T R E F O I L S ■
R ■ E ■ P ■ I ■ O ■ N ■ L ■
U ■ D O U B L E D I G ■ A ■
C ■ ■ R ■ L ■ I ■ ■ ■ ■ N ■
E L D E R S ■ A L M O N D
```

Puzzle 18

```
G A R D E N I N G ■ L ■ H
R ■ A ■ N ■ V ■ ■ H A L O
A ■ K ■ G ■ O ■ ■ R ■ U R
P ■ E ■ L A R G E ■ P ■ E
E ■ ■ I ■ Y ■ P ■ E ■ E ■
H E R B S ■ ■ L I L A C ■
Y ■ ■ H O S T A ■ ■ ■ C H
A S T E R ■ ■ C H I V E ■
C ■ U ■ O ■ D ■ E ■ ■ S ■
I ■ B ■ S C R U M ■ V ■ T ■
N ■ E ■ E ■ I ■ E ■ I ■ N
T U R F ■ ■ L ■ N ■ N ■ U
H ■ S ■ A L L O T M E N T
```

Puzzle 19

```
■ W A L L F L O W E R S ■
M ■ T ■ A ■ O ■ E ■ O ■ E
A ■ T ■ U N C L E ■ B O X
S H E A R ■ A ■ D ■ E ■ A
T ■ M ■ E ■ T ■ S E D U M
E S P A L I E R ■ ■ ■ ■ I
R ■ T ■ S ■ ■ C ■ S ■ N
P ■ ■ ■ V I O L E T T A
I N P U T ■ B ■ A ■ R ■ T
E ■ A ■ H ■ E ■ S A U D I
C A T ■ Y A R D S ■ D ■ O
E ■ I ■ M ■ I ■ I ■ E ■ N
■ H O N E Y S U C K L E
```

Puzzle 20

```
W H E E L B A R R O W ■ P
E ■ A ■ U ■ E ■ ■ Y ■ L
E ■ R ■ S ■ C H I C ■ A
D U T C H H O E ■ ■ H E N
I ■ H ■ E ■ D ■ ■ E ■ E
N ■ ■ A S S E M B L Y ■
G ■ P ■ ■ K ■ ■ M ■ G
■ L A D Y B I R D ■ ■ A
A ■ R ■ E ■ E ■ F ■ R
C O S ■ A L L R O U N D
O ■ ■ N E W T ■ A ■ G E
R ■ I ■ E ■ T ■ ■ G ■ N
N ■ P O I N S E T T I A S
```

Puzzle 21

Puzzle 22

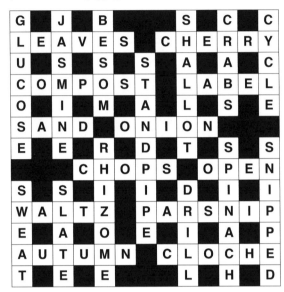

Puzzle 23

Puzzle 24

Puzzle 25

C	A	C	T	U	S	■	B	■	S	■	B	■
H	■	A	■	■	C	H	E	S	T	N	U	T
E	L	M	■	R	■	G	■	A	■	C	■	■
R	■	P	O	T	A	T	O	■	R	A	K	E
U	■	U	■	P	■	N	■	T	■	E	■	■
B	U	S	H	Y	■	V	I	O	L	E	T	S
■	■	E	■	V	■	A	■	E	■	■	■	■
H	A	N	D	S	A	W	■	A	D	O	R	N
■	R	■	G	■	N	■	R	■	■	R	■	E
K	A	L	E	■	I	G	U	A	N	A	■	T
■	B	■	R	■	L	■	S	■	■	N	U	T
F	L	O	O	D	L	I	T	■	■	G	■	L
■	E	■	W	■	A	■	S	P	H	E	R	E

Puzzle 26

L	E	I	N	S	T	E	R	■	■	B	E	E	T
E	■	N	■	T	■	X	■	■	X	■	U	■
E	L	D	E	R	■	T	A	G	E	T	E	S
K	■	I	■	I	■	E	■	■	■	O	■	S
■	■	G	■	M	■	N	O	V	E	L	L	O
B	L	O	O	M	E	D	■	E	■	S	■	C
I	■	■	I	■	■	G	■	■	K
N	■	M	■	N	■	S	P	E	C	I	E	S
D	R	O	U	G	H	T	■	T	■	N	■	■
W	■	W	■	A	■	A	■	F	■	A	■	■
E	T	E	R	N	A	L	■	B	E	A	N	S
E	■	R	■	K	■	L	■	N	■	K	■	■
D	U	S	K	■	A	S	B	E	S	T	O	S

Puzzle 27

A	P	P	L	E	■	S	C	Y	T	H	E	S
S	■	O	■	D	■	E	■	R	■	R	■	■
P	U	U	■	X	■	B	A	S	I	L	■	■
A	P	R	I	C	O	T	S	■	G	■	C	■
R	■	I	■	A	■	E	■	L	I	L	A	C
A	N	N	O	T	A	T	E	■	C	■	A	■
G	■	G	■	E	■	■	S	■	B	■	R	■
U	■	A	■	H	A	W	T	H	O	R	N	■
S	L	O	E	S	■	U	■	O	■	T	■	A
■	E	■	R	■	E	G	G	P	L	A	N	T
M	A	R	I	S	■	U	■	G	■	N	■	I
■	S	■	A	■	■	S	■	A	■	I	■	O
S	H	A	L	L	O	T	■	P	E	C	A	N

Puzzle 28

S	A	V	O	Y	■	P	U	M	P	K	I	N
P	■	A	■	A	■	U	■	■	L	■	B	■
E	■	N	■	R	■	R	■	B	A	S	I	L
A	P	I	A	R	I	S	T	■	C	■	Z	■
R	■	L	■	O	■	U	■	L	I	L	A	C
M	I	L	K	W	E	E	D	■	D	■	■	O
I	■	A	■	S	■	■	G	■	V	■	U	■
N	■	■	A	■	E	S	P	A	L	I	E	R
T	A	N	S	Y	■	H	■	R	■	S	■	G
■	I	■	L	■	W	O	O	D	B	I	N	E
O	T	T	E	R	■	W	■	E	■	B	■	T
■	C	■	E	■	E	■	N	■	L	■	T	■
C	H	O	P	P	E	R	■	S	W	E	D	E

Puzzle 29

Puzzle 30

Puzzle 31

Puzzle 32

Puzzle 33

Puzzle 34

Puzzle 35

Puzzle 36

Puzzle 37

S	L	O	E		W	A	T	E	R	I	N	G
A		A		C	U		N		T		R	
V	E	R	D	A	N	T		T	I	A	R	A
O		E		U		U		E		L		P
Y	O	D	E	L		M	O	R	T	I	S	E
C			I		N		T		C		H	
A	D	R	I	F	T		M	A	R	S	H	Y
B		E		L		E		I			A	
B	E	D	R	O	O	M		N	S	P	C	C
A		W		W		I		I		R		I
G	R	O	V	E		G	E	N	T	I	A	N
E		O		R		R		G		O		T
S	I	D	E	S	T	E	P		A	R	C	H

Puzzle 38

R	A	I	N	F	A	L	L		S	T	E	M
A		G		L		I					U	
K	E	N	D	O		C	H	I	T	S		L
E		I		W		H			A		B	
	T		E		E	S	S	E	N	C	E	
C	H	E	V	R	O	N		P		D		R
O		P				E				R		
P		U		O		S	A	V	O	R	Y	
P	I	N	E	T	U	M		R		I		
I		W			U		M		L		L	
C	H	E	R	V	I	L		I	S	S	U	E
E		L			C		N		E			
S	I	L	T		T	H	A	T	C	H		K

Puzzle 39

S	O	W		H	U	T		S	H	R	U	B
C		E			U		H		E		A	
R	O	T	S		K	N	E	E	L	E	R	S
U		L		O		N		A		D		K
B	L	A	C	K	B	E	R	R	Y			E
	N		R		L			F		T	
M	E	D	L	A	R		A	T	H	E	N	S
A		S			A		O		V	
L		L	A	W	N	M	O	W	E	R	S
L		B		E		N		L		R		L
O	D	Y	S	S	E	U	S		O	F	F	A
W		T		O		A			E		N
S	H	E	E	P		L	O	B		W	I	T

Puzzle 40

C	R	O	C	U	S		O		C		S
L		X			N	E	C	K	L	A	C	E
O	I	L		A		T		E		R	
C		I	N	D	I	G	O		M	E	E	T
H		P		L		B		A		E	
E	S	S	E	X		N	E	T	T	I	N	G
		S		N		R		I	
P	U	M	P	K	I	N		A	S	P	E	N
	P		A		G		S		E		E
O	R	A	L		E	S	T	I	M	A		T
	O		I		L		E			P	O	T
C	O	L	E	S	L	A	W			O		L
	T		R		A		S	A	D	D	L	E

Puzzle 41

```
S N O W D R O P . . . F I G S
A . N . I . R . . . C . . . W
C L I N G . A C O N I T E . .
K . O . I . C . . . C . . . E
. . N . T . . L E A F L E T .
M E S S A G E . . U . E . . P
A . . . L . . . . B . . . . E
I . E . I . F R E E S I A . .
N E M E S I A . R . . P . . .
C . B . . . T . G . A . . . T
R O L L E R S . . I N D I A .
O . E . . . I . . N . E . X .
P U M P . W A T E R S K I . .
```

Puzzle 42

```
B L U E B E L L . E C H O
I . X . V . . I . Q . E .
C L O C H E . M O U L D Y
Y . . E . N E E . I . G .
O P A L . I . S U N D E W
A . . . . N . . . O . . .
E D G I N G . L U X U R Y
. . . S . . . A . . . A .
S T O R E D . T . P U M A
I . A . R U E . . R . B .
F L E E C E . R O U B L E
T . L . A . . A . N . E .
T H A I . M U L B E R R Y
```

Puzzle 43

```
C H E F . C H I R P I N G
H . L . V . Y . H . C . R
R A B B I T S . O M E G A
Y . O . C . S . D . L . P
S O W . T O . . O V A T E
. . . . O . R . . . N . H
. . N E . R . E . D . . Y
. . T . V . I . D . N . .
H Y E N A . A . D . S A C
E . R . P . M . R . E . I
M E T A L . S N O W D O N
U . O . U . O . N . G . T
M O N U M E N T . M E S H
```

Puzzle 44

```
S E L E C T . . B . P E N
. X . . O . S I E V E . A
S H A L L O T . E . R . I
A . . . U . E . S U G A R
C U C U M B E R . . O . O
. S . . B . P . S . L . B
S T A T U E . W A S A B I
K . P . S . S . L . A . .
I . R . . W A T E R I N G
M O I S T . U . S . . K .
M . C . I . C O M P O S T
I . O X E Y E . A . . I .
A N T . S . . A N N U A L
```

Puzzle 45

S	P	U	D	S		M	U	L	C	H	E	D
P		N		E		A		O		R		
E		E		A		N		C	L	E	A	N
A	C	A	N	T	H	U	S		L		T	
R		R		T		R		J	A	C	O	B
M	O	T	E	L	I	E	R		R		L	
I		H		E			R		L		U	
N		L		D	R	A	I	N	A	G	E	
T	U	L	I	P		O		N		N		B
	S		L		F	O	X	G	L	O	V	E
C	U	M	I	N		T		L		L		R
	A		E			E		E		I		R
B	L	E	S	S	E	D		T	A	N	S	Y

Puzzle 46

S	A	L	A	D	S		P	R	U	N	E	R
T			I		O		I				E	
U		B	R	A	S	S	I	C	A	S		T
M		R		N		T		E		Y		U
P	L	A	N	T	A	I	N		A	C	E	R
S		N		H		A		M		A		F
	S	C	R	U	B		P	A	L	M	S	
C		H		S		D		G		O		S
I	R	I	S		L	E	O	N	A	R	D	O
T		N		H		L		O		E		R
R		G	L	A	D	I	O	L	U	S		R
U			W		A		I					E
S	Q	U	A	S	H		L	A	U	R	E	L

Puzzle 47

S	A	G	E		R	A	M	B	L	I	N	G
W		O		W		L		L		N		A
E	A	R	T	H	E	D		A	L	D	E	R
E		S		E		R		C		O		D
T	H	E	R	E		I	R	K	S	O	M	E
W			L		N		C		R			N
I	M	B	I	B	E		R	U	S	S	E	T
L		O		A		M		R				R
L	I	N	A	R	I	A		R	H	O	D	O
I		F		R		R		A		L		W
A	M	I	N	O		T	I	N	M	I	N	E
M		R		W		H		T		V		L
S	E	E	D	S	M	A	N		C	E	P	S

Puzzle 48

S	N	A	P	D	R	A	G	O	N		H	
C			O			E		I	R	O	N	
A	D	I	E	U		R		G		T		
M			G	R	A	E	M	E		H		
P		L		N		A	R	R	O	W		
I	B	I	Z	A		G		I		U		
	O		S	A	L	A	D			S		
T		F		I		E	L	D	E	R		
D	A	L	A	I		N					O	
N		B	R	A	N	C	H				D	
I		H		C		A	P	P	L	E		
O	S	L	O		I		I			N		
T		R	E	D	C	U	R	R	A	N	T	

Puzzle 49

```
S C O T S F I R   S P I T
A   L   W   N       R   R
C H I V E   S A T S U M A
K   V   E   E       N   N
    E   T   C H A F E R S
H A R I C O T   Q   D   F
Y     O     U     E
A   M   R   S H A R P E R
C A Y E N N E   D   A
I   R     A   U   M   S
N E T T L E S   L U P I N
T   L     O   C   A   O
H O E S   U N D E R S O W
```

Puzzle 50

```
  H O R S E R A D I S H   H
S   R   E   E   U   E   G
P   E   R O S E S   P E A
R O G E R   C   T   A   R
I   A   A   U   S O L I D
N I N E T E E N       E
G   O   E     F   D   N
O     G H E R K I N S
N Y M P H   E   E   B   P
I   A   E   R   T I B I A
O W N   R I B E S   L   D
N   G   O   A   A   E   E
  C O R N F L O W E R S
```

Puzzle 51

```
A   S   P     B   A   X
L O P P E R   J E R S E Y
P   I   O   A   G   P   L
I N N I N G S   O X E Y E
N   A   Y   P   N   N   M
E T C H   S A L I X
S   H   J   R   A   J   B
    J A P A N   B U R R
J   P   S   G   S   N   A
A S S A M   U R A N I U M
F   A   I   S   V   P   B
F E L I N E   B O R E A L
A   M   E     Y   R   E
```

Puzzle 52

```
D I G   C O S   S I E V E
A   E     O   H   R   N
T U R F   V A L E R I A N
E   T   T   K   A   C   O
S T R A W B E R R Y     B
    U   I   D     D   L
I N D I G O   F L E E C E
S   E     S   O   S
T     D E L P H I N I U M
H   C   D   I   S   G   A
M A H O G A N Y   S N I P
U   I   E   E     E   L
S I T A R   S A P   R U E
```

Puzzle 53

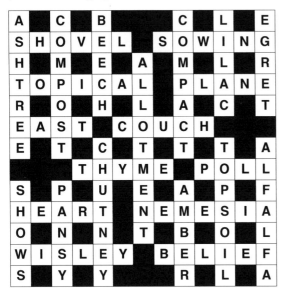

Printed in Great Britain
by Amazon